PRODIGAL SON

BOOKS BY JOHN PATRICK SHANLEY AVAILABLE FROM TCG

Defiance

Dirty Story and Other Plays
ALSO INCLUDES:
Where's My Money?
Sailor's Song

Doubt, a parable

Outside Mullingar

Prodigal Son

Storefront Church

PRODIGAL SON

―――――

JOHN PATRICK SHANLEY

THEATRE COMMUNICATIONS GROUP   NEW YORK   2016

Prodigal Son is published by Theatre Communications Group, Inc., 520 Eighth Avenue, 24th Floor, New York, NY 10018-4156

The publication of *Prodigal Son* by John Patrick Shanley, through TCG's Book Program, is made possible in part by the New York State Council on the Arts with the support of Governor Andrew Cuomo and the New York State Legislature.

TCG books are exclusively distributed to the book trade by Consortium Book Sales and Distribution.

Cataloging-in-Publication Data is on file at the Library of Congress, Washington, DC.

ISBN 978-1-55936-526-0 (paperback)
ISBN 978-1-55936-852-0 (ebook)

Book design and composition by Lisa Govan
Cover design by John Gall
Cover photo by Imelda Kahuni/EyeEm
Author photo by Monique Carboni

First Edition, March 2016

PREFACE

In 1965 I arrived, a very troubled youth, at a private school in New Hampshire called Thomas More Preparatory School. Fifty-five boys were sequestered on a five-hundred-acre reservation on a mountaintop, for the purpose of education. I was from the Bronx, rather violent, a bit delusional, hungry for all kinds of things, and wild-eyed as a rescue dog. The teachers were all male save one, the headmaster's wife, Louise Schmitt, and she taught one other boy and me in her home. Our subject was *The Waste Land*, and we studied it through a long winter and into the spring. I felt I didn't understand the poem, and I didn't care. I had seen a picture of T. S. Eliot, and I didn't like the look of him. He wasn't for me because I didn't want to *be* him. That was how I judged poets then.

This play is my account of that time, the period during which my whole life was being decided. It is a true story for the most part. The changes I've made have been to simplify or make a point.

Most of the names remain unchanged, or only slightly altered. I wish you could have been there. I wish more generally that you could have shared my whole life with me, so we could discuss and compare. These plays I write are the best I can do to make that possible.

—*JPS*

PRODIGAL SON

PRODUCTION HISTORY

The world premiere of *Prodigal Son* was produced by Manhattan Theatre Club (Lynne Meadow, Artistic Director; Barry Grove, Executive Director) in New York City on February 9, 2016. It was directed by John Patrick Shanley. The scenic design was by Santo Loquasto, the costume design was by Jennifer von Mayrhauser, the lighting design was by Natasha Katz, the sound design was by Fitz Patton and original music was composed by Paul Simon. The cast was:

JIM QUINN	Timothée Chalamet
MR. CARL SCHMITT	Chris McGarry
MR. ALAN HOFFMAN	Robert Sean Leonard
AUSTIN LORD SCHMITT	David Potters
LOUISE SCHMITT	Annika Boras

CHARACTERS

JIM QUINN

MR. CARL SCHMITT

MR. ALAN HOFFMAN

AUSTIN LORD SCHMITT

LOUISE SCHMITT

SETTING/PLACE

A boys' prep school in New Hampshire.

SCENE 1

Music establishes quiet tension. A spotlight. There's a paperback on the floor. Jim Quinn enters from the surrounding dark, picks up the book. He's in a white shirt, navy sports jacket, black pants, oxfords, skinny black tie. He's from the Bronx, and sounds it. He quietly says to the audience:

JIM: I always had a book. I was fifteen. Do you remember fifteen? For me, it was a special, beautiful room in Hell.

(More light. Sound of a train.)

I came by train. Mr. Schmitt and I met at a diner in Keene, New Hampshire. 1965.

(Carl Schmitt enters, crew cut, New England reserve, early forties, also in a jacket and tie. He and Jim sit in a diner booth. Carl

figures out Jim's credits on a napkin. They have a stainless steel pot of tea. Jim forgets the audience.)

MR. SCHMITT: Jim.

JIM: Mr. Schmitt!

MR. SCHMITT: I read your transcript, Jim. You've had a pretty bumpy two years.

JIM: Yes, I guess I have.

MR. SCHMITT: Can I ask you something?

JIM: Sure.

MR. SCHMITT: It says you were suspended for saying you didn't believe in God. Is that true?

JIM: It's true that I said it, but I didn't mean it.

MR. SCHMITT: Then why did you say it?

JIM: I just was trying to wake the teacher up. Brother Henry. He taught Religion, but the way he taught it, he just read from the book. He didn't like questions. So I raised my hand and said I didn't believe in God to see what he'd do.

MR. SCHMITT: And what did he do?

JIM: Well, it definitely woke him up, but he wasn't happy. He sent me to the principal.

MR. SCHMITT: It's a serious thing to say you don't believe in God, Jim.

JIM: That's what the principal said. He suspended me.

MR. SCHMITT: What got into you?

JIM: Just crazy stuff.

MR. SCHMITT: What?

JIM: Well, the thought came into my head to say I didn't believe in God, and I thought, "Who put that thought there?" And I thought it was probably God, you know?

MR. SCHMITT: What if it was the Other Guy?

JIM: I don't think so. I feel like the Devil would want me to be lazy, and God would want me to speak.

MR. SCHMITT: You're fifteen?

JIM: Yeah. Yes. I'll be sixteen in October.

MR. SCHMITT: I teach Religion. Comparative Religion. But unlike your friend Brother Henry, I don't read to the class from a book. I understand you attended a retreat this summer at my school, sponsored by Opus Dei.

JIM: Yes.

MR. SCHMITT: To see if you wanted to be a priest.

JIM: I didn't. I don't.

MR. SCHMITT: How'd you get involved with Opus Dei?

JIM: Mr. Benishek, my Political Science teacher brought me to their house. They kind of adopted me.

MR. SCHMITT: Lot of smart people at Opus Dei.

JIM: And The John Birch Society.

MR. SCHMITT: What's that?

JIM: Mr. Benishek. He took me to hear The John Birch Society, too. You know, a speaker.

MR. SCHMITT: What did you think?

(Jim laughs.)

JIM: Oh, he messed up.

MR. SCHMITT: In what way?

JIM: He said bad stuff about President Kennedy to a bunch of Irish Catholics in the Bronx. They almost lynched him.

MR. SCHMITT: But what did you think of the speaker?

JIM: I thought he was crazy. But I liked hearing what he said because I'd just never heard anybody talk like that. I like things I haven't thought of.

MR. SCHMITT: Is that why you went on the retreat?

JIM: Pretty much. I never really thought I'd be a priest. My mother'd like it.

MR. SCHMITT: You met a member of our faculty at the retreat. Alan Hoffman.

JIM: He told you about that?

MR. SCHMITT: He said you were very good at Charades.

JIM: He did?

MR. SCHMITT: He was amazed. Apparently you guessed *The Rubáiyát* of Omar Khayyám after one clue.

JIM: I really like that poem.

MR. SCHMITT: Why?

JIM: I don't know. I'd like to live like that guy.

MR. SCHMITT: You mean, drink a lot of wine?

(Jim laughs.)

JIM: No. He's just not . . . There's no misery, you know? You know that poem?

MR. SCHMITT: Sure.

JIM: He saw day and night like a chessboard, and God was a big finger writing in the sky. He just seemed to see things so . . . he saw the size of things. And he was free. Happy. He saw Time goes really fast. I think that, too. Life is so short.

MR. SCHMITT: If you only live in the physical, it is short, but some people think beyond their own lives. "The future's more beautiful than now."

JIM: It is?

MR. SCHMITT: A French theologian named Teilhard de Chardin said that. He believes that we're headed somewhere as a race, to a moment of epiphany. He calls it the Omega Point.

JIM: The Omega Point. Sounds like a science fiction movie.

MR. SCHMITT: Yes. So why do you think you did so badly in your last school?

JIM: I don't know. I felt like I was trying but I just couldn't do it. The building was ugly. All the classrooms, everything looked like a kitchen. It made me feel bleak.

MR. SCHMITT: Lot of students?

JIM: Yes.

MR. SCHMITT: Thomas More is different than that. The main building's an old mansion, and the student body is very small. Do you know who Thomas More was?

JIM: He was a martyr. He wouldn't lie about what he believed. So the king had him killed.

MR. SCHMITT: I'm surprised you didn't do better on the IQ test.

JIM: I used to do good on them.

MR. SCHMITT: Well.

JIM: Excuse me?

MR. SCHMITT: You used to do well on them.

JIM: Right. I used to do well on IQ tests. I think IQ tests make me nervous now.

MR. SCHMITT: Why?

JIM: I see how the questions could have a lot of different answers, and the answer choices never seem to include something I can completely agree with so it makes me feel like something is wrong. My brother Tom loved taking IQ tests. He's older than me.

MR. SCHMITT: What's he doing now?

JIM: Vietnam.

MR. SCHMITT: You proud of him?

JIM: Sure.

MR. SCHMITT: Well, the way I figure your credits, you can go into junior year.

JIM: I can?

MR. SCHMITT: Barely but yes. I'll give you a scholarship for the tuition, but your parents will have to pay for your room and board.

JIM: Is that a lot of money?

MR. SCHMITT: It's not too bad, no.

JIM: How much?

MR. SCHMITT: Nine hundred dollars.

JIM: Sounds like a lot.

MR. SCHMITT: Your mother said it was all right.

JIM: Well, she's the bookkeeper. Why would you give me a scholarship? I flunked everything.

MR. SCHMITT: I think you can do the work. And your mother cried on the phone.

JIM: She did?

MR. SCHMITT: A little.

JIM: She called from work, you know, 'cause it's free. She's a telephone operator.

MR. SCHMITT: Yes, I could hear the other operators in the background.

JIM: She'll be happy I have somewhere to go. She was pretty worried.

MR. SCHMITT: What about you?

JIM: I was pretty worried, too. Like I said. I had nowhere to go.

MR. SCHMITT: Well, make use of the opportunity. All right. I've got to get back. When does the train come?

JIM: In about two hours.

MR. SCHMITT: Not too bad. You'll be all right?

(Jim holds up a thick paperback.)

JIM: Sure. I have a book.

MR. SCHMITT: What is it?

JIM: *Interpretation of Dreams.* I got it across the street.

MR. SCHMITT: Sigmund Freud.

JIM: I started it. I like reading the dreams, not what they mean.

MR. SCHMITT: Why's that?

JIM: I think the dreams are really interesting, but when he says what they mean . . . I don't know. It doesn't ring a bell.

(Mr. Schmitt gets up and offers his hand.)

MR. SCHMITT: Well. See you soon.

JIM: Thank you, sir.

MR. SCHMITT: Very good. I'll call your mother.

JIM: Thank you.

(Mr. Schmitt goes. Jim drinks his tea, mellow, and comments quietly to the audience:)

And I thought, "Wow. I'm saved."

(He gets up.)

I stole this book.

(We hear ticking. Music. The main building appears. It's an old mansion repurposed as a school. Jim looks at it.)

That's the main building at Thomas More School. Harrisville, New Hampshire. Fall semester.

(Jim starts toward the building, then disappears.)

SCENE 2

The Headmaster's office appears. Mr. Schmitt goes to his desk, reading handwritten pages. There's a pendulum clock. The ticking stops. Something occurs to him. He looks at the clock. He mumbles, "Gosh darn it." He mounts a chair, fishes out a key, and winds the clock. A knock.

MR. SCHMITT: Come in.

> *(Alan Hoffman enters. He's a teacher, late thirties, warm smile, easy manner, floppy hair, soft New England accent, wears a lot of corduroy.)*

Hi, Alan.

MR. HOFFMAN: What are you doing up there, Carl? Is there a mouse?

MR. SCHMITT: Very funny.

MR. HOFFMAN: What you doing on the chair?

(Mr. Schmitt gets down.)

MR. SCHMITT: The clock stopped. It has to be wound every eight days. I always forget until I hear the silence.

MR. HOFFMAN: My clock has to be wound every day. Keeps me on my toes. You have a minute?

MR. SCHMITT: Sure. I was just reading the paper you left in my box. Jim Quinn's opus about the Nazis.

MR. HOFFMAN: Oh good. I wanted you to have that as background.

MR. SCHMITT: He has an unusual conscience. For a boy.

MR. HOFFMAN: He's an overheated adolescent who likes to get a rise out of people.

MR. SCHMITT: He sounds like he wants to dig Hitler up and kill him again.

MR. HOFFMAN: He writes very well.

MR. SCHMITT: He does. But I've heard from Rooney that he's failing Chemistry.

MR. HOFFMAN: Well, he's acing English.

MR. SCHMITT: That's his natural strength. Real discipline is overcoming your weak suit.

MR. HOFFMAN: You're right.

MR. SCHMITT: What's on your mind?

MR. HOFFMAN: Him. Have you seen his sweatshirt?

MR. SCHMITT: His sweatshirt?

MR. HOFFMAN: He's wearing a sweatshirt that says PRAY FOR WAR in big letters.

MR. SCHMITT: Really? No, I hadn't seen it.

MR. HOFFMAN: It offends me a bit but it makes Charly Ahern ashen, absolutely ashen. Can you imagine? PRAY FOR WAR.

MR. SCHMITT: Well, Charly was raised a Quaker.

MR. HOFFMAN: You don't have to be a Quaker to find PRAY FOR WAR offensive, Carl.

MR. SCHMITT: They make sweatshirts that say such things?

MR. HOFFMAN: It's homemade. His brother gave it to him.

MR. SCHMITT: His brother who's in Vietnam?

MR. HOFFMAN: Exactly. He's a Marine. It's his sweatshirt from when he was in combat training.

MR. SCHMITT: Have you said anything?

MR. HOFFMAN: Ordinarily I would have.

MR. SCHMITT: But?

MR. HOFFMAN: Jim is from such a different background.

MR. SCHMITT: Yes.

MR. HOFFMAN: Where he comes from . . .

MR. SCHMITT: The war is viewed as patriotic.

MR. HOFFMAN: Exactly.

MR. SCHMITT: You still teaching Wilfred Owen, e.e. cummings?

MR. HOFFMAN: Sure.

MR. SCHMITT: *Johnny Got His Gun, All Quiet on the Western Front*?

MR. HOFFMAN: Absolutely.

MR. SCHMITT: You have a point of view, Alan. You're a pacifist. It's legitimate. But you're the head of our English Department and I wonder if you stack the deck.

MR. HOFFMAN: I can't teach if I don't believe what I'm teaching.

MR. SCHMITT: There were a lot of reasons why I took James Quinn on. One reason was we don't have another boy like him. He's working class.

MR. HOFFMAN: He could be so much more than that.

MR. SCHMITT: Nothing wrong with a blue-collar background.

MR. HOFFMAN: Of course not.

MR. SCHMITT: He's entitled to wear the sweatshirt.

MR. HOFFMAN: He's here to be educated. Those attitudes will hold him back.

MR. SCHMITT: With certain people, perhaps.

MR. HOFFMAN: It's condescending to leave him in ignorance.

MR. SCHMITT: Of what?

MR. HOFFMAN: He's not a Neanderthal by disposition.

MR. SCHMITT: It's his brother's shirt. Who's risking his life for his country.

MR. HOFFMAN: It's a ridiculous war fought for reasons that make no sense.

MR. SCHMITT: To you.

MR. HOFFMAN: Do you think we should be in Vietnam?

MR. SCHMITT: People get worked up about politics, Alan. You're no exception. You're convinced of something and there's no point in my trying to talk you out of it.

MR. HOFFMAN: You're in favor of the war?

MR. SCHMITT: I'm here to educate a group of young men to the best of my ability and so are you. You're not here to win them over to your point of view. I'm interested in values. If we give these boys solid values, they will apply those values in ways we can't foresee and don't need to control.

MR. HOFFMAN: Good point.

MR. SCHMITT: Not that he's easy. He's in my Comparative Religion class, and he's become a little obsessed with Taoism. I usually spend ten minutes on it, but he's kept it alive for two days. I'm falling behind in my syllabus. Who knew ancestor worship was so fascinating?

MR. HOFFMAN: Taoism?

MR. SCHMITT: It makes a lot of sense to him for some reason. But the more I explain it, the more I'm concerned I may inadvertently be making a convert.

(Mr. Hoffman is amused.)

MR. HOFFMAN: Oh dear.

MR. SCHMITT: I had to remind him he's a Catholic.

MR. HOFFMAN: I wonder what that's about?

MR. SCHMITT: I don't know. Kids get their enthusiasms.

MR. HOFFMAN: He's hit a couple of boys.

MR. SCHMITT: I know. They teased him about his accent. I doubt they will again. I want you to watch out for him.

MR. HOFFMAN: I don't mind.

MR. SCHMITT: He's the most interesting mess we have this year.

MR. HOFFMAN: He looks up to you.

MR. SCHMITT: Let's keep it that way. My chief weapon as headmaster is to stay mysterious. I can't be his friend, but you can.

MR. HOFFMAN: I'd be delighted.

MR. SCHMITT: But refrain from brainwashing.

MR. HOFFMAN: Of course.

MR. SCHMITT: You're good with the troubled ones.

MR. HOFFMAN: Sometimes. I wish I'd been able to help Niccolo.

MR. SCHMITT: Niccolo's problems were beyond all of us. He's better off with his family.

MR. HOFFMAN: I suppose.

MR. SCHMITT: Thank God he didn't know where his artery was.

MR. HOFFMAN: Well, he did fail Biology.

MR. SCHMITT: What?

MR. HOFFMAN: Joke.

MR. SCHMITT: Yes. As far as Jim goes, let him find his way. I'm hopeful he will. If he needs to be disciplined, I'm here.

MR. HOFFMAN: Very good.

MR. SCHMITT: Have you seen this movie, *The Birds*?

MR. HOFFMAN: Alfred Hitchcock?

MR. SCHMITT: It was on TV last night. Scared the stuffing out of me.

MR. HOFFMAN: I haven't seen it.

MR. SCHMITT: Stands everything on its head. Nature gets possessed of this evil intelligence. I woke up yelling. Louise had to explain to me there were no birds in the house.

MR. HOFFMAN: Where do they come up with these ideas?

MR. SCHMITT: I made a connection to the school. I feel some kind of blight running through the student body. That boy Tom Hendricks was staring at me the other day like a dog would. I don't like to look at a boy and think of an animal. It unsettled me.

MR. HOFFMAN: Hendricks is a bit of a numbskull.

MR. SCHMITT: Louise tells me it's my imagination. That my natural primitive fear of death got hold of me. But that didn't strike a chord. My only fear of death is that I'll be separated from Louise. What good would Heaven be without her?

MR. HOFFMAN: What a wonderful thing, to feel like that about someone.

MR. SCHMITT: Yes. I wish it on you.

MR. HOFFMAN: Some day perhaps.

MR. SCHMITT: For the sake of balance, have you considered teaching a pro-war book?

MR. HOFFMAN: Carl.

MR. SCHMITT: I can't think of a good one, anyway.

(The lights fade as Mr. Schmitt disappears and Mr. Hoffman walks into darkness. The clock chimes nine times.)

SCENE 3

The lights come up on a funky dorm room. Two single beds. Out the window, it's snowing. Here we find Jim and Austin, both sixteen. Jim is ringing a large brass bell with a clapper. Austin is a gangly, confident kid who is utterly himself: humble and gregarious. He has a New England accent and wears round black glasses. Jim addresses the audience:

JIM: Here ye! Here ye! Here ye! I was sixteen. Winter of '66.

(He forgets us and rings the bell again.)

AUSTIN: Quiet! Quiet! You're going to bring down the forces on us, man. That bell is loud.
JIM: I'm done. I just had to ring it.
AUSTIN: Where'd you steal it?
JIM: I didn't steal it.

AUSTIN: Where'd you get it?

JIM: A house on Silver Lake. It wasn't even locked really. Same place I got this.

(Jim pulls out a half full bottle of brandy from behind his bed.)

AUSTIN: Oh man, what's that? Don't tell me. You're going to get us killed.

(Jim takes a slug and offers it to Austin.)

JIM: Apricot brandy.

AUSTIN: Not for me.

JIM: Just taste it.

(Austin takes a sip.)

AUSTIN: Whoa.

JIM: Right? I don't even like apricots, but that is good.

AUSTIN: It's spreading out in my chest. My stomach feels like a lightbulb.

JIM: Summertime in a bottle.

(Jim takes another slug and throws himself on his bed.)

"Give me a ship and a star to steer her by!" Man, do I like understand that.

AUSTIN: That from a poem?

JIM: Yeah.

AUSTIN: You love that stuff.

JIM: What do you love?

AUSTIN: Math?

JIM: Why?

AUSTIN: Because it makes sense.

JIM: I think I should change my name to Siegfried Sassoon.

AUSTIN: Was he somebody?

JIM: A poet.

AUSTIN: You like his stuff?

JIM: I just like his name. Siegfried Sassoon. James Quinn. What kind of boring name is that?

AUSTIN: You think your name is boring? How about Austin Schmitt?

JIM: Austin Lord Schmitt.

AUSTIN: I think it sucks.

JIM: I'm guessing you were named after Alfred Lord Tennyson.

AUSTIN: You're right. My mom loved Alfred Lord Tennyson so I'm Austin Lord Schmitt.

JIM: You have a good name. Want to hear a poem?

AUSTIN: No.

JIM: Shut up. It's short.

AUSTIN: Okay.

JIM: "The German drew back his knife. He saw the Jew Man's strife. He asked, Where is your God now, Jew? The Jew replied, He's in your knife, which is about to run me through."

AUSTIN: You're still on the Nazis?

JIM: What do you think of the poem?

AUSTIN: You want to know the truth? I think it's deep.

JIM: Don't bullshit me.

AUSTIN: Could you not curse so much? I think it's deep for real.

JIM: Why?

AUSTIN: I don't know. Where's this stuff come from?

JIM: I don't know. You think it's good?

AUSTIN: Yeah. But enough about the Nazis, Jim. Everything reminds you of the Nazis.

JIM: Yeah, you're right.

AUSTIN: Do you ever write about anything else?

JIM: I wrote this today. Ready?

AUSTIN: No. I'm not ready.

JIM: Shut up. "Adam, standing buck naked and stock still, / Listened quietly to the dew as it settled. He stood chilly, and damp, and quite alone. A half of a man with a fiery, aching rib."

AUSTIN: That's it?

JIM: Yeah.

AUSTIN: That's Adam from the Bible, right?

JIM: Yeah. It's about loneliness. He's the only person in the world. Everything's good, but he's the only person in the world.

AUSTIN: Is it about you?

JIM: I don't know.

AUSTIN: I'll tell you right out. I'm not embarrassed. I miss my mom.

JIM: But when you're with your mom, are you still lonely then?

AUSTIN: No, why would I be? I'm with her.

JIM: Right. What about the other loneliness?

AUSTIN: I don't know what you're talking about.

JIM: When you're home with your family, don't you get lonely then, too?

AUSTIN: Sometimes.

JIM: So what's that loneliness?

AUSTIN: Romantic.

JIM: Right.

AUSTIN: I'd like a girlfriend.

JIM: I'm looking at you. I think you're shit out of luck.

AUSTIN: Eat me. Do you have a girlfriend?

JIM: No. Well. There's Linda Pepe, *(Pronounces it "Peppy")* but I blew that.

AUSTIN: Who's she? What did you do? Take your time. I want details.

JIM: She came into my class in eighth grade. Italian. And she was a woman. You know what I mean?

AUSTIN: Like how?

JIM: She was busting out of her clothes, and her eyes were black, glittery black, and everything she did was black magic. She never moved in a way that wasn't worth watching. I could watch her all day.

AUSTIN: So what happened?

JIM: She asked me to walk her home one day, and I realized she liked me.

AUSTIN: How did you know?

JIM: Because she asked me to walk her home.

AUSTIN: And that made you know she liked you?

JIM: Yeah.

AUSTIN: So you walked her home?

JIM: No.

AUSTIN: Why not?

JIM: What I did was, I knocked her books out of her hands and laughed at her.

AUSTIN: What? Why?

JIM: I don't know. And that was the end of that.

AUSTIN: Maybe you can still patch it up?

JIM: No. I'm not even there. Anyway, I knew what would happen if I walked her home.

AUSTIN: What?

JIM: It would be, you know . . . It wouldn't be what I wanted.

AUSTIN: What did you want?

JIM: A big situation. A staircase.

AUSTIN: You wanted a staircase?

JIM: Linda Pepe couldn't *be* Linda Pepe. She was too wrapped up in passing for an ordinary girl. She didn't know what she was.

AUSTIN: What was she?

JIM: She was twenty feet tall. She was beautiful. Not pretty. Not cute. Beautiful. But she didn't know it. She didn't want to know it, in my opinion, and that made me so mad I knocked her books out of her hands and let her hate me.

AUSTIN: I wish you walked her home. You wish you walked her home.

JIM: Maybe yeah. *(Takes another drink)* "I am the master of my fate, / I am the captain of my soul."

AUSTIN: That another poem?

JIM: Not by me. I wish I felt like that.

AUSTIN: Like what?

JIM: Like I was the master of my fate.

AUSTIN: What would you do?

JIM: I'd smoke. I'd drink. I'd hitchhike all over the country. Catch fish, eat corn from the cornfields, write poems like Walt Whitman just naming everything. And I'd punch anybody who bothered me. Pow! Right in the face. I'd fight in wars and say everything that came into my head. I'd travel through time, too, and meet all the geniuses. Wouldn't that be cool?

AUSTIN: Yeah, it's impossible though.

JIM: It's a prison to think things are impossible.

AUSTIN: Okay. I'd like to meet Sir Isaac Newton.

JIM: He'd be good. And Beethoven.

AUSTIN: And Pablo Picasso.

JIM: You don't need a time machine to meet Picasso. He's still alive.

AUSTIN: No. He must be dead a long time.

JIM: Nope. His picture was in the paper around Thanksgiving.

AUSTIN: For what?

JIM: For just still being alive I guess. And I'd like that, too. To be super old. And famous. Like in a Chinese robe and sunglasses.

AUSTIN: I can't picture you old.

JIM: I can't picture me right now. Maybe I'm going crazy.

AUSTIN: You are not.

JIM: Everything I do, I don't know why I do it. I'm like a robot. I don't know why I took that bell. Do you feel like you're missing everything?

AUSTIN: Sure.

JIM: Why?

AUSTIN: Because I am. I'm on top of a mountain in New Hampshire in a tiny boys' school run by my freaking uncle.

JIM: Do you wish you were in Vietnam?

AUSTIN: No.

JIM: Me neither.

AUSTIN: I thought you said you wanted to fight in wars?

JIM: Not that war.

AUSTIN: Why not?

JIM: It's the wrong kind of real. And it's too small.

AUSTIN: So what war would be good?

JIM: I don't know. Maybe I want to be French.

AUSTIN: You do not. The French can't fight.

JIM: Are you serious? Have you ever heard of Napoleon Bonaparte?

AUSTIN: Right. Okay.

JIM: Yeah, I want to be French. I'll wear a cool hat and fight the Spanish.

AUSTIN: Are the French and the Spanish even fighting?

JIM: Not now.

AUSTIN: Did they ever?

JIM: They fought back when there were swords. Back in the seventeenth century.

AUSTIN: Well, you can't fight in the seventeenth century.

JIM: Why not?

AUSTIN: 'Cause it's impossible.

JIM: So what! And I think you're wrong. And I want my girlfriend to bring food and flowers and wine, right in the middle of the battle, and we have a dinner party while the bombs rip through everything.

AUSTIN: Linda Pepe.

JIM: Yeah, I want Linda Pepe to love me so much she doesn't want to live if she can't feed me, even though there's a war.

AUSTIN: You are the craziest person I've ever met.

JIM: Then you should meet more people. I want her to be rich. I want her to be covered with diamonds in a dress with blue stars. And she gets it dirty and torn just to visit me on the battlefield.

AUSTIN: Man, they're going to take you away.

JIM: Where would they take me? The way people see things is so stupid. It's a jail and I want out. I want to bust out.

AUSTIN: You're not going to have to bust out. You're going to get thrown out if they find that bottle. We both are. You'd better get rid of it.

JIM: I will.

AUSTIN: Soon.

JIM: When I'm ready.

AUSTIN: I'm serious. My uncle is a hard-ass. He will kick you out. You're not back on the block now.

(Jim is stung.)

JIM: What do you mean? Like sippin' Ripple?

AUSTIN: What?

JIM: I'm not back on the block sippin' Ripple?

AUSTIN: What are you talking about?

JIM: I'm talking about sippin' Ripple or T-bird or Bali Hai, downin' some shit wine back on the block. You think you're better than me?

AUSTIN: Who said that?

(Jim attacks Austin, pins him down.)

JIM: You! Say it! What do you think? You're better than me? Huh? Or your uncle? Who's he? Who died and left him king? Nobody's better than me! This is America.

AUSTIN: Get off me!

JIM: No! You four-eyed retard! When are you going to stop
fudging your underwear?

AUSTIN: Get off!

JIM: You're never going to get a girlfriend.

AUSTIN: You douche!

JIM: Are you going to tell about the bell?

AUSTIN: No!

JIM: You'd better not! I'll beat you to death! I'll turn into a dog
and bite your face!

(Austin shoves him off.)

AUSTIN: What's the matter with you? You're a complete asshole!

JIM: You're all right.

AUSTIN: Don't drink anymore.

JIM: I wasn't going to.

AUSTIN: Do you want me to ask for another roommate? 'Cause
I will.

JIM: No. I'm sorry I jumped you.

AUSTIN: What are you calling me a retard for? What's wrong
with you?

JIM: I've been called a retard plenty of times. Back on the block.
I didn't like that back on the block crap.

AUSTIN: I didn't mean anything by it.

JIM: I'm worried that it's all written down, okay? That I have
no say. I don't know why I do things. It's creepy. It drives
me nuts. Am I taking orders? From who? The whole thing
makes me feel like a slave.

AUSTIN: Come on. Jim, you're a teenager.

JIM: What does that mean?

AUSTIN: It isn't going to stay like this.

JIM: You know that?

AUSTIN: Of course.

JIM: So all these years, sixteen years, it's okay if they're wasted?

AUSTIN: Take it easy. Are you crying?

JIM: No.

AUSTIN: Hey, man, it's okay.

JIM: I'm sorry. You're such a better person than I am. You deserve a better roommate than me.

AUSTIN: Just get rid of the bottle.

JIM: Okay. After lights out. *(Pause)* I have a sword, you know.

AUSTIN: What are you talking about?

JIM: I have a sword.

AUSTIN: I don't see a sword.

JIM: No? "For the sword outwears its sheath, / And the soul wears out the breast, / And the heart must pause to breathe, / And love itself have rest."

AUSTIN: What's that?

JIM: Lord Byron. *(Touches his breast)* He was saying there's a sword here, and it's going to wear away everything else. I feel that.

AUSTIN: Talk more about Linda Pepe.

JIM: I don't really have more.

AUSTIN: I knew an Italian girl. Her name was Maria Mazzola. She was at the same day camp as me. Whenever she sat down, she folded her hands on one knee. Like this. I'd wait for her to do it. It was so cool. The folded hands. It was like she was a queen on her day off. I used to think about her and say her name when I was alone. Maria Mazzola. I'd write it on an envelope like I was going to send her a letter, but I didn't even know her at all. She was just this girl I would see at camp. And then one day she was gone. She got sick or something, and I never saw her again. But I still say her name sometimes.

JIM: Maria Mazzola.

AUSTIN: Maria Mazzola.

JIM: Maria Mazzola.

AUSTIN: Linda Pepe.

JIM: Not as good. Maria Mazzola is better. At the top of a flight of stairs she waits, listening for the words that will win her love.

AUSTIN: What would you say to her?

JIM: Maria, I am nothing. I have nothing. I'm poor, and the world does not know me. But if you let me into your heart, you will not be sorry. If you decide to let me into your crystal castle, I will face down the Nazis for you.

AUSTIN: Wow. The Nazis again.

JIM: I know. I can't help it. They're everywhere.

AUSTIN: What would you do if Maria like, came down the stairs?

JIM: She never comes down the stairs. Never. Or I'm not ready for her to come down the stairs. I'm a beggar in the dark. Lights out.

(The lights have been fading through the end of the scene. And now it is dark. Silent.

Eerie music plays through into the next scene.)

SCENE 4

Mr. Hoffman appears out of the dark with a flashlight. He addresses us as if we were the boys:

MR. HOFFMAN: Everybody up and everybody outside! Louie, wake him up. Throw on a coat. Sorry to hustle you out of your rooms, gang, but there was no way around it. Someone at Carriage House has been stealing Connell's record albums and we have to put a stop to it. Two seniors will enter each of your rooms and do a search. There's nothing to worry about unless you're the thief. If anyone wants to tell me something, now's the time. Once the student responsible has been exposed, there's nothing I can do for you. This shouldn't take more than half an hour. Anyone who needs to can approach me during that time. Again, I'm sorry you have to go through this.

(The scene cross-fades to:)

SCENE 5

The Headmaster's house. A recording of The Waste Land *plays over music. Louise Schmitt, thirty-seven, sits at a table reading* The Waste Land. *Her hair and clothes are styled like that of WWII. Scarf at the neck. She's quite self-possessed. There's a dining table that doubles as a desk. On the table are some papers and a tea set. The phone rings. She gets up and answers it.*

LOUISE: Hello? No? All right, I'll manage. Thank you, Wally.

(The doorbell rings.)

Oh here's the other one. I will. *(To the door)* Come in.

(She hangs up, opens a door, and Jim comes in. He's wearing a scarf.)

Hello, James.

(Jim takes off his construction boots.)

JIM: Hello, Mrs. Schmitt. I'm sorry I'm late. Mr. Boadway *(Rhymes with "roadway")* needed some help. The van was stuck.

LOUISE: That van is always getting stuck. It's all right. William has the flu, so you're the sole student in English Honors today. Would you like some tea?

JIM: Yes, thank you.

LOUISE: Cookies?

JIM: No, thank you.

LOUISE *(Serving tea)*: Did you read *The Waste Land* through to the end?

JIM: I didn't understand it.

LOUISE: That's why we're here.

JIM: I read it four times.

LOUISE: It bears repeating readings.

JIM: I felt like he was a professor showing off how smart he was. And that maybe he was drunk.

LOUISE: I think T. S. Eliot was a rather sober man.

JIM: When I read old poems, like the old English poems Mr. Hoffman assigns, they don't seem old. But when I read *The Waste Land*, it seems old to me.

LOUISE: But it was written in the modern era.

JIM: I don't think anybody's going to read it in a hundred years.

LOUISE: Why not?

JIM: I don't know. I looked at his picture. He looks like an undertaker. I think a poem that won't be good in a hundred years, isn't good now.

(She chuckles, despite herself.)

LOUISE: Well, I think I should wait to discuss it till William's with us. Since there's only the two of you. Can you meet tomorrow after second period?

JIM: Sure. I wrote a poem. I'd like to get your opinion. Can I read it? It's short.

LOUISE: All right.

JIM: "The German drew back his knife. He saw the Jew Man's strife. He asked, Where is your God now, Jew? The Jew replied, He's in your knife, which is about to run me through."

LOUISE: May I see it?

(He gives it to her.)

You forgot quotation marks.

JIM: Yeah, I did without.

LOUISE: Quotation marks can be helpful. They avoid confusion. Who's the speaker?

JIM: Me.

LOUISE: God's in the Nazi's knife?

JIM: Yes. God kills the guy. God's responsible.

LOUISE: Are you saying the Nazi is not responsible?

JIM: People are born somebody. They don't choose who they are. I was born me. I don't get to be somebody else, even if I want to be somebody else.

LOUISE: Do you want to be somebody else?

JIM: What's it matter? I can't be. I'm Jim Quinn. I was born Jim Quinn and I'll die Jim Quinn.

LOUISE: But you have a free will.

JIM: But the free will I have is mine because I'm me. The choices I make I make because I'm Jim Quinn. And that I didn't choose. Personality is everything really. I think.

LOUISE: But you do believe we have a free will?

JIM: I don't know. I want to believe it. What do you think of the poem?

LOUISE: I like things about it. Your tea is getting cold. It has compassion for the Jewish man.

JIM: What about the Nazi?

LOUISE: What about him?

JIM: The Jewish guy gets to be right. The Nazi is more like people really are. They suffer because they're wrong.

LOUISE: Most people don't want to murder Jews.

JIM: People do stuff and don't know why. The Nazis were crazy, but they didn't know it. They thought they'd figured it all out. It takes the victim to school the killer on what's what. The only way I know anything about how I am is what I see in other people's eyes. If I pick my nose and I'm alone, I don't know it's disgusting. I think the Jew makes the Nazi see. Which would tick me off if I was the Nazi. It's hard to hear you're a Nazi. You know what? I don't think I'm making any sense.

LOUISE: You're doing all right.

JIM: This isn't a very good poem.

LOUISE: It's not bad.

JIM: There's something I want to say, but I can't say it. I think *The Waste Land* is about going into the desert, and that I identify with. I know we're not talking about it till tomorrow.

LOUISE: I know that life can be confusing. Especially for the young.

JIM: Are you confused?

LOUISE: Not especially. But then I'm not especially young.

JIM: "The dead tree gives no shelter."

LOUISE: What's that?

JIM: It's a line in *The Waste Land*. "The dead tree gives no shelter."

LOUISE: What about it?

JIM: That line gives me a pain.

LOUISE: But why? It's a beautiful line.

JIM: Who cares if it's beautiful? What somebody should have told that guy was that the tree isn't dead. Plain and simple.

LOUISE: How do you know that?

JIM: I know.

LOUISE: But how?

JIM: Life doesn't die. What would you think if I changed my name to Rafael Sabatini?

(Louise is distracted by what Jim just said about life.)

LOUISE: What? Who's that?

JIM: He wrote *Scaramouche*.

LOUISE: And what's that?

JIM: A great book. The first line is "He was born with the gift of laughter and a sense that the world was mad."

LOUISE: Nice.

JIM: They made it into a movie. It has the greatest sword fight in history.

LOUISE: What's the name again?

JIM: Rafael Sabatini. "I am Rafael Sabatini."

LOUISE: But if that was your name then you'd be Italian.

JIM: Or Siegfried Sassoon.

LOUISE: The poet?

JIM: Yes.

LOUISE: What's wrong with James Quinn?

JIM: Come on. What is James Quinn when compared with Rafael Sabatini or Siegfried Sassoon?

LOUISE: I think James Quinn is a fine outline and it's up to you to fill it in.

JIM: I think my parents named me to work in the Sanitation Department.

LOUISE: I like the name James. What did you mean, you identified with the idea of going into the desert?

JIM: In the Bible, when people go into the desert, they meet God or the Devil, or both. And then they choose. 'Cause it's the Bible they choose God. But in real life, they choose the Devil just as much.

LOUISE: Because they have a free will.

JIM: Wow. You got me. Good one.

LOUISE: You write about the Nazis a lot.

JIM: I'm done with it I think. Yeah, I'm done.

LOUISE: Why have you found them so interesting?

JIM: They're just the perfect enemy.

LOUISE: I see. That makes sense.

JIM: It does?

LOUISE: Yes. It's clear. They're bad.

JIM: They make you answer them.

LOUISE: What's that?

JIM: When they say they're Nazis, you have to say who you are.

(Pause.)

LOUISE: Who are you?

(Pause.)

JIM: What if you did something wrong?

LOUISE: Like what?

JIM: I don't know.

LOUISE: Did you do something wrong?

JIM: No.

LOUISE: You seem like you have something on your mind.

JIM: I feel like Elfego Baca.

LOUISE: Someone else I haven't heard of. I feel so uninformed.

JIM: Elfego Baca was a Spanish cowboy. He was in a shootout in New Mexico. It was him against eighty men. They shot at him four thousand times. But they never got him.

LOUISE: Elfego Baca.

JIM: Yeah. They called him "The man with nine lives." He could survive anything. What if you stole a bunch of records from another kid, and you wanted to give them back.

LOUISE: Then you'd give them back.

JIM: But everybody's in an uproar about these records being stolen. They made everybody in Carriage House stand outside last night while they searched our rooms. How could I give them back without getting thrown out?

LOUISE: Is this why you want to change your name?

JIM: No. I don't know.

LOUISE: What is it about those names you like so much?

JIM: They're the names of heroes. "I am Rafael Sabatini. Do your worst."

LOUISE: You want to be a hero, Jim?

JIM: I guess, but I can't now.

LOUISE: You can start any time.

JIM: That's not true. The moment you can be a hero, that's a day that comes your way, or it doesn't.

LOUISE: Give back the records. Admit what you did.

JIM: I can't. I want to, but I can't. I can't be myself yet.

LOUISE: Why not?

JIM: Because the news isn't good. If I'm put on the spot to tell the truth, the truth needs to be good. Heroes tell the truth because they have something great to say, and once they say it, who cares? It's okay to die. That's why they can face down death. Like Thomas More.

LOUISE: You want to be like Thomas More?

JIM: I don't think so, but I'd like to be like somebody. If they find out it was me that took the records, they'll throw me out.

LOUISE: You mean my husband?

JIM: Yes.

LOUISE: He might.

JIM: He will.

LOUISE: What would you do if you got thrown out?

JIM: Go back to the Bronx.

LOUISE: Would that be so bad?

(The opening music plays. The lights change.)

JIM: Help me.

(Louise busies herself, preparing for dinner. As she walks off to the kitchen, Jim exits. A car's headlights pass through the room. Louise walks into:)

SCENE 6

The dining room. Louise clears the dining table, sets it for dinner. Carl Schmitt enters. Louise greets him, kissing his cheek. She returns to her preparations as Carl hangs up his coat. Louise brings in dinner and Carl helps her serve it. He pulls out a chair for Louise and she sits. He sits. The music concludes. They bow their heads and say grace:

MR. SCHMITT AND LOUISE: In the name of the Father, the Son, and the Holy Ghost. Bless us, O Lord and these thy gifts which we are about to receive from thy bounty through Christ our Lord.

LOUISE: Amen.

(Carl goes on a beat longer, then raises his head.)

MR. SCHMITT: Amen.

LOUISE: I always know when you take extra time with grace you're troubled.

MR. SCHMITT: Smells good.

LOUISE: You know why?

MR. SCHMITT AND LOUISE: Because it is good.

MR. SCHMITT: Did you read that piece on John Rock?

LOUISE: Yes. I think you should get him up here to talk to the seniors.

MR. SCHMITT: Maybe.

LOUISE: He has one of the most exciting minds in the Catholic community.

MR. SCHMITT: He's a romantic. For a scientist, that's not ideal.

LOUISE: He understands women, I'll tell you that much. Which is more than I can say for a lot of them.

MR. SCHMITT: Count me among the ignorant.

LOUISE: I do. "A woman should be absolute mistress of her own body."

MR. SCHMITT: Yes. Could you not quote Margaret Sanger at the dinner table?

LOUISE: You quote Teilhard de Chardin, and I think he has mush for brains.

MR. SCHMITT: At least he was devout.

LOUISE: Don't be dogmatic.

MR. SCHMITT: I was born dogmatic.

LOUISE: Sanger's hardly a bomb thrower. She was invited to speak at Vassar.

MR. SCHMITT: She's an atheist.

LOUISE: Even on a good day, Chardin was a heretic.

MR. SCHMITT: Sanger's awful and you know it.

LOUISE: Agreed, but nobody's perfect.

MR. SCHMITT: You are.

LOUISE: Fight fair. All right. Let's drop the debate. How was your day?

MR. SCHMITT: I'm sorry I'm out of sorts. It was a darned strange day.

LOUISE: How so?

MR. SCHMITT: I had Carriage House searched the other night. It's distasteful, but there's been a rash of thievery, and I wanted to put a stop to it. No discoveries were made, but this morning, the missing items showed up in the faculty lounge.

LOUISE: Well, I guess somebody's conscience kicked in.

MR. SCHMITT: But no student has the key to that room, which means a faculty member was involved.

LOUISE: What would you have done if you caught the boy?

MR. SCHMITT: It was Jim Quinn.

LOUISE: Are you sure?

MR. SCHMITT: No. But it was him. Alan Hoffman told me as much.

LOUISE: And how does Alan know?

MR. SCHMITT: He knows kids. What do you think of Jim?

LOUISE: Well.

(She ponders.)

MR. SCHMITT: What is it?

LOUISE: I think he's good.

MR. SCHMITT: You do?

LOUISE: Yes.

MR. SCHMITT: Why?

LOUISE: We were talking about *The Waste Land* and he said he understood what it is to be in the desert. He was speaking spiritually. He is honestly struggling, Carl.

MR. SCHMITT: His struggle is taking up a lot of room.

LOUISE: Something told you to take him in.

MR. SCHMITT: It's not working out.

LOUISE: Are you being lazy?

MR. SCHMITT: No.

LOUISE: I sometimes think you're only an idealist because it's easier.

MR. SCHMITT: What's easy about idealism?

LOUISE: Ideals do the work for you. It's thoughtless. You don't have to allow for human frailty.

MR. SCHMITT: Louise?

LOUISE: Yes?

MR. SCHMITT: Did you open the lounge and put those things in there?

LOUISE: Yes.

MR. SCHMITT: Well, mystery solved at any rate.

(He starts eating. She waits. He says no more.)

LOUISE: Is that all you have to say about it?

MR. SCHMITT: If you chose to help the boy, that's enough for me. I'll leave it be.

LOUISE: Every time I think you can't surprise me, you do.

MR. SCHMITT: Glad to be of service.

LOUISE: Sometimes I wonder how I found you.

MR. SCHMITT: It wasn't hard. I was pining away outside your dormitory.

LOUISE: He's using poetry like a ladder to climb out of some terrible place.

MR. SCHMITT: What place?

LOUISE: I don't know. I think where he comes from must be hard.

MR. SCHMITT: Is the poetry any good?

LOUISE: Yes, but that doesn't matter.

MR. SCHMITT: Point taken. How was your day?

(Louise becomes quietly emotional.)

LOUISE: I need a ladder like that too, some days. I wish I had one.

MR. SCHMITT: I saw you this morning, looking out the window.

LOUISE: I'm sorry.

MR. SCHMITT: What for? You have been a wonder.

LOUISE: It's been two years.

MR. SCHMITT: I know.

LOUISE: Today.

MR. SCHMITT: I know.

LOUISE: You could've said something.

MR. SCHMITT: I don't know what to say.

LOUISE: He hates Emily Dickinson.

MR. SCHMITT: Who?

LOUISE: Jim. He made such fun of "There is no frigate like a book" that I don't think I can ever read that poem again without laughing.

MR. SCHMITT: It's not her best work.

LOUISE: Stop teaching.

MR. SCHMITT: Done.

LOUISE: How do any of us survive?

MR. SCHMITT: Love.

MR. SCHMITT: Maybe we should . . .   LOUISE: Carl.

MR. SCHMITT AND LOUISE: What?

MR. SCHMITT: Nothing.

LOUISE: Fine.

(They disappear. We hear ticking. Beethoven's Sonata No. 17 "The Storm" plays.)

SCENE 7

Mr. Hoffman's study. The Beethoven piece continues until Mr. Hoff-man lifts the needle on his turntable. Jim is singing. Jim and Mr. Hoffman play chess.

JIM:

> She'll be coming around the mountian when she comes
> She'll be coming around the mountian when she comes . . .

I keep thinking about that thing Heraclitus said.

MR. HOFFMAN: Which thing is that? "You can't step into the same river twice"?

JIM: No. "Character is destiny."

MR. HOFFMAN: That is pithy, but is it true?

JIM: Is it?

MR. HOFFMAN: I think so. They called Heraclitus the Weeping Philosopher.

JIM: What was he weeping about?

MR. HOFFMAN: He didn't like people very much.

JIM: I can understand that, but . . . I like people.

(Jim makes a move.)

MR. HOFFMAN: You sure you want to do that?

JIM: I took my hand off it.

(Mr. Hoffman takes his castle.)

MR. HOFFMAN: There goes your rook. Did you have a chance to read Phaedrus?

JIM: I couldn't remember which one you said, so I read Phaedo and Phaedrus. Yeah. It's almost over my head, but Socrates was incredible.

MR. HOFFMAN: How so?

JIM: He wasn't afraid of anything. I couldn't drink poison.

MR. HOFFMAN: He had the courage of his convictions.

JIM: Right. In a way, I don't get it. All he had to do was say what they wanted and everything would've been okay.

MR. HOFFMAN: That's right.

JIM: But because of his personality, he couldn't.

MR. HOFFMAN: I wouldn't put it that way.

JIM: Heraclitus would.

MR. HOFFMAN: Touché.

JIM: I wish Socrates didn't die like that.

MR. HOFFMAN: It was kind of beautiful.

JIM: I wish he died after eating spaghetti or something.

MR. HOFFMAN: Why?

JIM: I like spaghetti.

MR. HOFFMAN: Socrates should not have died eating spaghetti.

JIM: I mean, he was a suicide.

MR. HOFFMAN: Not really.

JIM: Yes, he was. Same as Thomas More.

MR. HOFFMAN: Thomas More was not a suicide. He had his head chopped off. He was a martyr.

JIM: But what does that mean? He made the king kill him. Jesus was a suicide, too, really.

MR. HOFFMAN: Egad! Jesus was not a suicide.

JIM: Yes, he was.

MR. HOFFMAN: He was crucified.

JIM: Because he wouldn't play the game and lie about what he believed.

MR. HOFFMAN: Exactly.

JIM: "Thou shalt not lie" isn't even one of the commandments.

MR. HOFFMAN: "Thou shalt not bear false witness against thy neighbor."

JIM: Nobody was asking Jesus to rat out his neighbor, just back off the King of the Jews stuff.

MR. HOFFMAN: Jesus was not a suicide.

JIM: Socrates, Jesus, Thomas More, all those stories are the same. Why should you help the killers kill you? Why even give the truth to second-rate people who don't deserve it?

MR. HOFFMAN: We all deserve the truth.

JIM: Why?

MR. HOFFMAN: Because it's important that a hero lead the way.

JIM: Jesus Christ was no hero like I think of a hero. Heroes fight for life. Jesus just handed them his sword and said, "Kill me."

MR. HOFFMAN: For heaven's sake, Jim, whatever you do, don't say something like that about Jesus Christ in front of Mr. Schmitt.

JIM: Why not?

MR. HOFFMAN: Just don't.

JIM: Okay.

MR. HOFFMAN: He won't appreciate it. If you want to talk about your philosophy of heroism, do yourself a favor and confine it to Socrates.

JIM: Socrates had some ideas I don't even know what to think of them.

MR. HOFFMAN: Like what?

JIM: He says we should talk about things because it makes us remember stuff we were born knowing, but forgot. Do you believe that?

MR. HOFFMAN: I don't know.

JIM: Me neither.

MR. HOFFMAN: Socrates prepared for death his whole life. That's why he was good at it.

JIM: Do you do that?

MR. HOFFMAN: I try.

JIM: I don't. No, I do actually. I'm always facing the Nazis. And if I tell them the truth, they'll kill me.

MR. HOFFMAN: So what do you do?

JIM: So far, I just face them. I open the door and they're there, staring at me. And I think: "Am I going to tell them the truth and be destroyed?"

MR. HOFFMAN: You have the most remarkable mind.

JIM: I do?

MR. HOFFMAN: It's a little scary.

JIM: Are you bullshitting me?

MR. HOFFMAN: Maybe. *(Smiles)* So. Do you know what Phaedrus is really about?

(Jim makes a move.)

JIM: Check.

MR. HOFFMAN: You bastard. Good one. Socrates is trying to seduce Phaedrus with the beauty of his thoughts.

(Jim acts as if he knew, but he didn't and he's uneasy.)

JIM: Oh yeah.

MR. HOFFMAN: You got that?

JIM: Yeah.

MR. HOFFMAN: It's pretty amusing when you read it that way.

JIM: Right.

(Mr. Hoffman takes Jim's queen.)

MR. HOFFMAN: There goes your queen.

JIM: Oh man.

MR. HOFFMAN: Do you want to concede?

JIM: No.

MR. HOFFMAN: What are you going to do on summer vacation?

JIM: I got a job.

MR. HOFFMAN: Good for you. Doing what?

JIM: Unloading trucks.

MR. HOFFMAN: Cool.

JIM: With my dad. I want to apply to Harvard.

MR. HOFFMAN: Bad idea.

JIM: Why?

MR. HOFFMAN: It's Carl Schmitt's alma mater. He only submits, tops, two boys for Harvard each year, so they'll take our applications seriously, and you just don't have those grades.

JIM: Oh.

MR. HOFFMAN: Sorry.

JIM: I thought you thought I might have a chance.

MR. HOFFMAN: It's not up to me. I think you're extraordinary, but Harvard is not in the cards. You just don't have the grade-point, Jim.

JIM: I guess. There's no law against me filling out the application though.

MR. HOFFMAN: Not a good idea. Have faith that I know whereof I speak. Try for NYU.

JIM: Okay.

(Pause.)

MR. HOFFMAN: The truth is: Mr. Schmitt has reservations about you.

JIM: What do you mean?

MR. HOFFMAN: Let's leave it at that.

JIM: How can I leave it at that?

MR. HOFFMAN: He suspects that you were the thief at Carriage House.

JIM: He does?

MR. HOFFMAN: I tried to dissuade him, but that's the story.

JIM: It wasn't me.

MR. HOFFMAN: I believe you. It's just that you were really artificially casual that night.

JIM: I was not.

MR. HOFFMAN: Look, Jim, I think the world of you. People make mistakes. But if there's something weighing on you, for your own good, you might want to unburden yourself.

JIM: I wish you didn't put it to me like that.

MR. HOFFMAN: I think you want to talk.

JIM: You won't tell?

MR. HOFFMAN: I'm on your side.

(Jim fights crying.)

JIM: Okay. It was me.

(Jim throws himself into Mr. Hoffman's arms.)

MR. HOFFMAN: It's okay. It was obvious.

JIM: It was?

MR. HOFFMAN: Oh my God yes.

JIM: Do people know?

MR. HOFFMAN: Nobody knows for sure.

JIM: What should I do?

MR. HOFFMAN: Nothing. Connell got his stuff back. Given time, the whole thing will blow over.

JIM: You won't tell?

MR. HOFFMAN: You're safe.

JIM: Thank you.

MR. HOFFMAN: You'll go home this summer, and when you come back as a senior, all this will be forgotten.

JIM: You think so?

MR. HOFFMAN: Yes. You just need to stop screwing up, and go ahead and have a great senior year. Can you do that?

JIM: Sure. So you think NYU's my best bet?

MR. HOFFMAN: It's a fine choice.

JIM: Do you think you'd have time to help me with the application?

MR. HOFFMAN: Of course. And I'll write you a wonderful recommendation.

JIM: Thank you. I wish I knew Socrates.

MR. HOFFMAN: He would've liked you.

JIM: I'll tell you this much. I would've talked him out of dying.

(Jim and Mr. Hoffman walk away in opposite directions. Lights cross-fade to:)

SCENE 8

Jim, drunk, appears in moonlight with a bottle of whiskey in his hand. He is singing "She'll Be Coming 'Round the Mountain." He dances a bit, clutches his stomach, and runs off. We hear him retching.

SCENE 9

A classroom. A portable blackboard. Jim enters, pale and tired. He speaks quietly to the audience:

JIM: I was seventeen. Spring of 1968.

> *(Jim sits at his desk and starts writing in a blue book.)*

MR. SCHMITT *(Entering)*: How you doing, Jim?

JIM: Fine.

MR. SCHMITT: Feeling all right?

JIM: Better.

MR. SCHMITT: Don't worry. This doesn't come off your exam time. I've stopped the clock.

JIM: I'm almost done.

MR. SCHMITT: Don't rush. You may not have to finish.

JIM: I'm sorry I missed the final. I just got sick.

MR. SCHMITT: It's been a long year, Mr. Quinn. You've made it a very long year.

JIM: What do you mean?

MR. SCHMITT: Two years really. Almost. Nine days to graduation.

JIM: Yeah.

MR. SCHMITT: Do you think you should graduate?

JIM: Yes.

MR. SCHMITT: Do you know why I started this school?

JIM: No, sir.

MR. SCHMITT: Because I wanted to turn out fine young men. Do you consider yourself a fine young man?

JIM: I don't know.

MR. SCHMITT: There was that break-in last year over at Silver Lake. Not that long after you joined us. Remember when I asked you about that?

JIM: I didn't do it.

MR. SCHMITT: And then Connell's record collection went missing.

JIM: I didn't touch his records. They searched my room.

MR. SCHMITT: Yes, they did. Were you drunk last night?

JIM: No.

MR. SCHMITT: The school nurse thought you were drunk.

JIM: I was sick.

MR. SCHMITT: I threw Bickford out at Christmas for smoking marijuana. I think maybe I should've thrown you out, too.

JIM: For what? I didn't do anything. And you didn't just throw out Bickford. You threw out half my dorm.

MR. SCHMITT: They were using drugs.

JIM: Well, I wasn't.

MR. SCHMITT: You didn't get caught.

JIM: Because I didn't take anything.

MR. SCHMITT: Some boys have been sent home this year that were of a higher caliber than you, Jim. Enough clouds have gathered around you where it's clear to me you've done more than enough to merit expulsion.

JIM: I haven't done anything.

MR. SCHMITT: Are you seriously saying that?

JIM: Look. Please don't throw me out, Mr. Schmitt.

MR. SCHMITT: Why shouldn't I?

JIM: Why should you?

MR. SCHMITT: You know what I don't understand? You're a cheat. You're close to incapable of telling the truth. But your work, there you have areas where it's clear to me that you're driven by the very highest ideals. How can that be?

JIM: You've read my essays?

MR. SCHMITT: Yes. I've read them all.

JIM: Why?

MR. SCHMITT: Because I'm trying to make a determination.

JIM: This place has helped me a lot.

MR. SCHMITT: I don't believe you. You've beaten up half the freshman class. You are widely disliked. I'm not a psychiatrist. What would you do if you were me?

JIM: I don't know. I'd let me stay.

MR. SCHMITT: My wife thinks your poetry is very good. Some of it.

JIM: She does?

MR. SCHMITT: Why are you acting surprised? She told you.

JIM: I guess I didn't believe her.

(Mr. Schmitt thinks.)

MR. SCHMITT: You're from the Bronx.

JIM: Yeah.

MR. SCHMITT: What's that like?

JIM: I don't know. Normal. Like anywhere else.

MR. SCHMITT: Were you in fights?

JIM: Sure.

MR. SCHMITT: New Hampshire must be a big change.

JIM: It's quiet.

MR. SCHMITT: Maybe I should call your parents.

JIM: They're not going to be able to tell you anything.

MR. SCHMITT: If I call them, it will be to tell them to come and take you home.

JIM: Please don't do that.

MR. SCHMITT: You've shown no particular desire to protect your place here.

JIM: What do you want me to do?

MR. SCHMITT: I don't know but you'd better think of something, Jim, because you're nine days from graduation and I don't see you getting a diploma.

JIM: I'm passing my courses.

MR. SCHMITT: There's more to this school than grades. Character is an issue.

JIM: What do you want me to say?

MR. SCHMITT: I don't know.

JIM: Mr. Hoffman thinks I'm worth it.

MR. SCHMITT: Worth what?

JIM: The trouble I guess.

MR. SCHMITT: I've talked to Mr. Hoffman.

JIM: What did he say?

MR. SCHMITT: He thinks you should graduate.

JIM: Well, shouldn't that count?

MR. SCHMITT: It's my decision. Alan often chooses a project, and this past year or so, it's been you. His judgment is colored by your work in his class. You're his star.

JIM: I'm doing so much better than I was. I failed everything in my last school.

MR. SCHMITT: Yes, and I took you in.

JIM: And I'm passing everything now.

MR. SCHMITT: Why couldn't you pass at Cardinal Spellman? Were you stupid then and smart now?

JIM: No I was always smart. Cardinal Spellman was stupid. I just couldn't do it. I just couldn't listen to them.

MR. SCHMITT: Who?

JIM: The teachers.

MR. SCHMITT: Why not?

JIM: They were just so boring. They were depressing. I felt like I was going crazy. I wrote stuff. I thought it was cool but I got in trouble for that. So I stopped showing them anything, and I just read all the time. But I didn't read what they told me to read, so that was a problem. They sent me to a psychologist . . . Anyway, here, Mr. Hoffman, when I talked about books, when I wrote stuff, he thought it was good. And he thought I was good.

MR. SCHMITT: Was he right?

JIM: You don't think I'm good.

MR. SCHMITT: Convince me otherwise.

JIM: What if I'm not?

MR. SCHMITT: Then I don't want you here.

JIM: That's not the way it works, you know. First you need to think I'm good, then I'm good. That's the real way things are.

MR. SCHMITT: What are you talking about?

JIM: How to deal with people.

MR. SCHMITT: So you know how to deal with people? The faculty is up in arms over your existence! And anyway, what do you mean? I should say you're good before you're good? How does that work? You're here to get an education. What do you think, that you should get an A before the class starts?

JIM: I think I should've gotten an A the day I was born.

MR. SCHMITT: For what?

JIM: For being alive.

MR. SCHMITT: Using that logic, I should have awarded you a diploma the day you got here.

JIM: The day before I got here.

MR. SCHMITT: Are you crazy?

JIM: Not that crazy.

MR. SCHMITT: Don't you think giving you a scholarship for nothing was enough?

JIM: It wasn't for nothing. You gave it to me because I needed it.

MR. SCHMITT: Exactly.

JIM: Well, I still need it.

(Mr. Schmitt thinks.)

MR. SCHMITT: What do you read?

JIM: I don't know. All kinds of stuff. Amazing things. Everything.

MR. SCHMITT: Why?

JIM: Because I love it. Because the dead tell me everything. Because the stiffs I actually have for teachers are so cheap. Except for Mr. Hoffman.

MR. SCHMITT: What do you mean, cheap?

JIM: Teachers don't tell you what they tell you in books. Charles Dickens tells you everything. Henry Miller tells you everything. Teachers tell you about other people, never themselves. You teach Religion, but I don't know anything about religion from you. I've never seen your soul. I've never met your God.

MR. SCHMITT: That's an unusual thing to say.

JIM: Why did you give me a scholarship?

MR. SCHMITT: I thought you could do the work.

JIM: That's not why. You gave me an IQ test. I didn't break a hundred.

MR. SCHMITT: IQ tests don't tell the tale.

JIM: Why'd you give me a scholarship?

MR. SCHMITT: Mr. Hoffman met you on that retreat.

JIM: So?

MR. SCHMITT: He put in a good word for you. He was impressed about your ready knowledge of *The Rubáiyát* of Omar Khayyám.

JIM: So Omar Khayyám got me in.

MR. SCHMITT: If you like.

JIM: It was Omar Khayyám. A dead guy.

MR. SCHMITT: Did he tell you to get drunk?

JIM: I didn't get drunk.

MR. SCHMITT: Jim, no one can know another man's God.

JIM: That's not true, Mr. Schmitt. I know Dostoevsky's God. Lots of other people. Homer. Even Einstein. But if you have a God, he sure as hell hasn't show up in your Religion class.

MR. SCHMITT: Watch your language.

JIM: This is so unfair.

MR. SCHMITT: What do you want? I'm giving you a chance to explain yourself.

JIM: What about you? Why don't you have to explain yourself?

MR. SCHMITT: It's my school.

JIM: Right. You're the guy. I'm on trial.

MR. SCHMITT: What would you call fair?

JIM: If it goes one way, I leave the school. If it goes the other, *you* leave. That would be fair. That's fair. This is just you having everything.

MR. SCHMITT: What are you talking about? It's my school. You're here because I've given you an opportunity.

JIM: Why is it your school? Why am I always in the wrong? Why do I have to listen to you when you have zero to say? Because I'm young? All my life I've been young. So I never get a turn? This school is lost, if you ask me. You're lost. But everybody talks to me like I'm the one. I should change. Why should I change? I've never even gotten to find out who I am and you want me to change? That's crazy! You tell me I'm bad before I even get to be anything. What the hell is that? Original sin or something? I read Plato. I read him on a park bench in the Bronx and let me tell you something. Plato wasn't afraid. Diogenes wasn't afraid. Socrates wasn't afraid of anything. They were men. Why are you the headmaster and I'm the student? Do you understand? I have to earn your respect but you don't have to earn mine? What is that? It's you that wants the A before you even start. But when I say I want the same thing, I'm nuts, right? I'm not going to cry. I'm going to find my place in this world. Count on it. This school has been a miracle for me, but not because of you. Because somebody, Mr. Hoffman, finally *saw* me. And more than that. Somebody, a grown person, decided I was good *before I was good*. You want to throw me out of that? Then you know what I say: I've never met your God and I don't want to.

MR. SCHMITT: Okay. That was impressive. You can express yourself. I respect that. It doesn't mean you're exempt from anything. We can't stay in the Gardens of Academe till nightfall discussing and reinventing civilization. We have to deal with the challenge at hand. What about Jesus Christ?

JIM: What about him?

MR. SCHMITT: This is a Catholic school. It's not just about grades. I have to protect the student body from moral peril.

JIM: Do you think I'm evil?

MR. SCHMITT: Are you?

(Jim makes a mental calculation and grudgingly offers.)

JIM: Jesus Christ had good ideas.

MR. SCHMITT: He was divine. *(Silence)* Do you know that?

JIM: Yes.

MR. SCHMITT: Do you want to have a good life, Jim?

JIM: Yes.

MR. SCHMITT: You've got to tell the truth.

JIM: About what?

MR. SCHMITT: Did you get drunk?

(Pause.)

JIM: No.

(Mr. Schmitt gets up and goes to the door.)

MR. SCHMITT: Finish your test.

(Mr. Schmitt goes. Jim sits down and continues writing in the blue book. He finishes. He breaks his pencil. Then he gets up and writes "Fuck You" on the blackboard. He returns to the desk. Mr. Hoffman enters. He crosses to Jim. Jim is subdued.)

MR. HOFFMAN: Time's up.

JIM: I'm done.

MR. HOFFMAN *(Referring to the blackboard)*: Oh God. When did this appear?

JIM: After Mr. Schmitt left.

MR. HOFFMAN: What did Mr. Schmitt say?

JIM: He said he was thinking of refusing to graduate me.

MR. HOFFMAN: Did he say you wouldn't graduate?

JIM: No.

MR. HOFFMAN: Jim. You have to behave with perfect rectitude between now and graduation.

JIM: Okay.

MR. HOFFMAN: I'm serious.

JIM: I know.

MR. HOFFMAN: Carl is one inch from throwing you out.

JIM: I hate him.

MR. HOFFMAN: He's a good man.

JIM: He doesn't make any, you know . . . He doesn't try to understand anybody.

MR. HOFFMAN: You're mistaken.

JIM: He looks at me like I'm disgusting.

MR. HOFFMAN: That's not accurate.

JIM: Have you talked with him about me?

MR. HOFFMAN: Of course.

JIM: What's he say?

MR. HOFFMAN: He's impressed that Louise likes you.

JIM: His wife?

MR. HOFFMAN: He values her opinion very highly.

JIM: I didn't think she liked me.

MR. HOFFMAN: She does.

JIM: Why?

(Mr. Hoffman smiles.)

MR. HOFFMAN: No accounting for taste.

JIM: What?

MR. HOFFMAN: Joke.

JIM: Oh.

MR. HOFFMAN: What are you going to do after you graduate?

JIM: If I graduate.

MR. HOFFMAN: You have to graduate.

JIM: Right.

MR. HOFFMAN: You just have to keep your head down for the next nine days. You can do that.

JIM: Yeah. *(Pause)* What do you think is going to happen to me? I mean, you know, what could I do for a job?

MR. HOFFMAN: You might become a social thinker, a working-class writer on union issues. Something like that. Or a journalist. Crime.

JIM: Why not a man of letters?

MR. HOFFMAN: All right. A man of letters.

JIM: A poet.

MR. HOFFMAN: Certainly you could be a poet.

JIM: You're just saying what I want to hear.

MR. HOFFMAN: I am not. You can succeed by writing, by going to college.

JIM: Come on. I haven't even been accepted anywhere.

MR. HOFFMAN: It's early.

JIM: Half the class has heard. More than half.

MR. HOFFMAN: You have a very promising future.

JIM: That's vague

MR. HOFFMAN: Stop.

JIM: Tell me about me. Please.

MR. HOFFMAN: You don't need me to do that.

JIM: Yes, I do.

MR. HOFFMAN: You just feel like you don't know yourself. It's not true.

JIM: Please, Alan. Tell me what I am.

MR. HOFFMAN: Well. You're an insightful reader.

JIM: Am I good-looking?

MR. HOFFMAN: Oh, is that what we're doing? Yes, you are good-looking.

JIM: I don't know anything. All I've got to go on is what other people say. I look at Mr. Schmitt and I think I'm bad. And ugly. Like no girl could ever want me. I'm worried I'm going to be a bum. I feel deformed.

MR. HOFFMAN: You're very handsome.

JIM: In comparison to the other guys here how am I?

MR. HOFFMAN: If you were being graded on your looks, you'd get an A.

JIM: Really?

MR. HOFFMAN: Yes. Doesn't your mother tell you that?

JIM: My mother? No. Like what would Lorenzo get?

MR. HOFFMAN: He'd get a C.

JIM: How about Woodruff?

MR. HOFFMAN: An A.

JIM: Fitzmaurice?

MR. HOFFMAN: Henry would get a D.

JIM: And I'd get an A?

MR. HOFFMAN: Yes.

JIM: I can't wait to go home.

MR. HOFFMAN: Why?

JIM: I gotta get out of here. I want people to see what I've become. Then I'll know. Have I changed since I've been here?

MR. HOFFMAN: Oh yes.

JIM: How?

MR. HOFFMAN: You're more sophisticated.

JIM: You mean . . . What do you mean by that?

MR. HOFFMAN: Your responses to literature have more depth.

JIM: You think they're going to notice that in the Bronx?

MR. HOFFMAN: Probably. Not directly, but you carry yourself with more confidence.

JIM: I need to have changed.

MR. HOFFMAN: You have.

JIM: I've got to be out of this part of my life.

MR. HOFFMAN: Why?

JIM: Because it's awful.

MR. HOFFMAN: What's important for you right now is to consciously address your behavior.

JIM: What do you mean?

MR. HOFFMAN: Among other things, your violence.

JIM: What do you mean?

MR. HOFFMAN: You have to stop hitting the freshmen.

JIM: I just kid around.

MR. HOFFMAN: They don't see it that way.

JIM: Who complained? Fitzmaurice?

MR. HOFFMAN: You have nine days. Don't drink. Don't smoke. Don't hit anybody. Don't steal anything.

JIM: Okay.

MR. HOFFMAN: Don't do anything. Make it through. We've worked too hard to blow it now.

JIM: Okay. Why have you helped me?

MR. HOFFMAN: I haven't done that much.

JIM: Come on. I would've been out the door if it wasn't for you.

MR. HOFFMAN: You deserve to be saved.

JIM: Some kids don't?

MR. HOFFMAN: Since the day you got here, you've been trying to achieve something. I respect that.

JIM: What?

MR. HOFFMAN: You want to shine.

JIM: Shine? I don't want to shine. I want to be great.

MR. HOFFMAN: All right.

JIM: I want to be great. I do. I want to be a great man.

MR. HOFFMAN: Then you will be.

JIM: I don't know, but I've got to try. Otherwise, why was I even born?

MR. HOFFMAN: Everybody doesn't think that way. Many of the boys here are just marking time.

JIM: Rich kids.

MR. HOFFMAN: It has nothing to do with money. You're one of the desperate ones.

JIM: That doesn't sound good.

MR. HOFFMAN: Maybe it isn't. Niccolo was like that.

JIM: The kid who tried to kill himself?

MR. HOFFMAN: He was unstable.

JIM: Am I unstable?

MR. HOFFMAN: No. You're strong. Maybe too damn strong. You're an extraordinary person, but guess what? A lot of kids are extraordinary and go absolutely nowhere. They take and take and never learn that life is a two-way street.

JIM: Are you starting to hate me, too?

MR. HOFFMAN: No, but I'm frustrated. You need to wake up.

JIM: To what?

MR. HOFFMAN: Your own worth. Your own beauty.

JIM: I don't understand.

MR. HOFFMAN: I know.

JIM: What do you see that they don't see? Why do you see it and nobody else does?

MR. HOFFMAN: Because I'm paying attention.

JIM: Mr. Schmitt is paying attention! He stares at me like death.

MR. HOFFMAN: You misread him.

JIM: What's he thinking?

MR. HOFFMAN: Okay. I'm going to tell you something. Something I have no business telling you. Do you know Mr. Schmitt lost a child?

JIM: What?

MR. HOFFMAN: Two years ago, he was plowing the road and he didn't see his little boy there. Carl Schmitt accidentally killed his son.

JIM: Jesus Christ! That's horrible.

MR. HOFFMAN: Yes, it is.

JIM: So his wife lost her kid?

MR. HOFFMAN: She looks out the window. You'll see her there from time to time. Just waiting for the child to come home I guess. Trust me. You don't know what Carl Schmitt is thinking when he looks at you. Nobody does. He's a complicated man.

JIM: Should you have told me that?

MR. HOFFMAN: Probably not.

(Mr. Hoffman touches Jim's face.)

JIM: What're you doing?

MR. HOFFMAN: Nothing.

(Mr. Hoffman leans in to kiss Jim. Jim reacts.)

JIM *(Barks)*: DON'T TOUCH ME!

(Jim throws Mr. Hoffman's hand off.)

MR. HOFFMAN: You need to be careful, mister.

JIM: Me?

MR. HOFFMAN: Don't you ever dare bark at me that way.

JIM: You made me nervous.

MR. HOFFMAN: That's no excuse to behave like a brute.

JIM: I'm not a brute.

MR. HOFFMAN: "PRAY FOR WAR."

JIM: It was my brother's shirt.

MR. HOFFMAN: But you wore it.

JIM: I don't anymore. I've changed.

MR. HOFFMAN: Well, good. Listen, you are a valuable person, Jim.

JIM: Why don't I know that?

MR. HOFFMAN: I don't know, but you'd better realize it before you throw it all away like you almost did last night, right? Right?

JIM: I didn't mean to get drunk.

MR. HOFFMAN: So you admit it. You got drunk.

JIM: Somebody hid a bottle under some rocks, one of the guys I guess, and out of the whole woods, I found it.

MR. HOFFMAN: And you drank it.

JIM: I just did. There it was, you know? I didn't plan it. I feel like all the trouble I get in, I don't plan it. Trouble just finds me.

MR. HOFFMAN: That's why you have to become aware.

JIM: Of what?

MR. HOFFMAN: You have power over things, Jim. That bottle of liquor. It has no life, volition of its own. You're what animates your world. You need to understand that, or you'll just keep feeling helpless and wreaking irresponsible havoc.

JIM: I'm sorry I yelled at you.

MR. HOFFMAN: No, you're not. You just want me on your side. You think everything's coming at you, when what's really happening is everything's coming *from* you. You're not the devastation. You're the explosion.

JIM: How can you be sure?

MR. HOFFMAN: Because I've gone through it. I've caused a lot of harm in my day.

JIM: Be more specific.

MR. HOFFMAN: No. Good luck.

(Mr. Hoffman starts to exit. Jim's next words stop him.)

JIM: Is that what happened with Niccolo? Is that why he had to go home?

MR. HOFFMAN: I think you're upset.

JIM: Come on, I've known people like you.

MR. HOFFMAN: Where? In the Bronx?

JIM: Yes.

MR. HOFFMAN: Don't lump me in with that crew.

JIM: You think you're better? Well, you're not. I gotta give it to you. You run an ice-cold game, sir. You're a cold customer.

MR. HOFFMAN: Fine. You think I'm cold? You haven't seen cold. I'll show you cold.

(Mr. Hoffman walks out. Jim stands, dejected. Ticking of a pendulum clock.)

SCENE 10

The Headmaster's office. Jim enters and sits in the visitor's chair. The ticking of the clock continues. Mr. Schmitt enters and sits behind his desk.

MR. SCHMITT: So here we are.

JIM: Yeah.

MR. SCHMITT: You know why I called you to my office?

JIM: Not exactly.

MR. SCHMITT: Mr. Hoffman tells me you've confessed to being intoxicated.

JIM: What? Mr. Hoffman what?

MR. SCHMITT: He said you told him you'd gotten drunk.

JIM: Mr. Hoffman told you that?

MR. SCHMITT: Yes.

JIM: When?

MR. SCHMITT: Today.

(Jim stamps his foot.)

JIM: The day before graduation.

MR. SCHMITT: Yes. Is it true you drank alcohol?

JIM: Yes, I got drunk.

MR. SCHMITT: Now that you've admitted you broke the school policy about alcohol, I'm not sure that I have any choice here.

JIM: You have a choice.

MR. SCHMITT: Tomorrow is graduation.

JIM: Yes.

MR. SCHMITT: The straw that broke the camel's back. Do you know that expression?

JIM: I know it. We just have to make it to tomorrow.

MR. SCHMITT: We?

JIM: Yes. Mr. Schmitt, is character destiny?

MR. SCHMITT: Absolutely not. That would be predestination and you don't believe in that.

JIM: I don't?

MR. SCHMITT: No, Catholics don't believe in predestination, and you are a Catholic. So you have a choice.

JIM: Then *you* have a choice.

MR. SCHMITT: Yes, I do.

JIM: About me. About whether or not I graduate. You are making me who I am right now. Right now.

MR. SCHMITT: What? How am I doing that?

JIM: You know what I'm taking about.

MR. SCHMITT: I have no idea what you're talking about. Morality can only come from you.

JIM: No. Morality is everybody together. I don't know much, but I know that.

(The clock stops. The lights change. Mr. Schmitt notices, looks at the clock.)

MR. SCHMITT: The clock stopped.

MR. HOFFMAN: Carl.

AUSTIN: Uncle Carl.

(Mr. Hoffman, Austin and Louise appear at the margins of the scene.)

LOUISE: Carl.

(Mr. Schmitt argues with her.)

MR. SCHMITT: No Louise, the alcohol rule applies to every student.

LOUISE: Don't be lazy.

MR. SCHMITT: There's nothing lazy about it.

LOUISE: You're an idealist because it's just easier!

MR. SCHMITT: This school will go out of existence in a few years. I'll shut it down because of my disappointment with the students here.

JIM: You're wrong. The school's here.

MR. SCHMITT: It's gone. I'm gone.

JIM: No. We're in it. Everything that ever happened is still happening.

MR. SCHMITT: That's impossible.

JIM: So what?

LOUISE: Carl.

MR. SCHMITT: Louise, the boy's gotta go. There's no way.

JIM: There is a way. There is a staircase.

LOUISE: A staircase?

AUSTIN: I see it, too!

JIM: Austin!

LOUISE: I don't see a staircase.

JIM: It's here. It starts where we are and goes someplace better.

AUSTIN: And Maria Mazzola is up there!

JIM: And Omar Khayyám!

AUSTIN: And Linda Pepe!

JIM: Mr. and Mrs. Schmitt, T. S. Elliot was wrong.

LOUISE: *The Waste Land* is a worthy poem, Jim. Reread it.

JIM: No. The tree is alive. Life doesn't die. I'm sixty-four, Mr. Schmitt, and you're dead, but I have a time machine and I can speak to great people who are gone. That's the gift I have been given and I thank God for it. We're all dead or about to be dead or we will never die because the human mind is a leaping spark. I know it! I do worship my ancestors. They're here right now. They make me understand and hunger for greatness. Still. Still.

LOUISE: Greatness is in the eye of the beholder, Jim.

MR. HOFFMAN: Greatness is an antiquated concept.

JIM: Greatness goes by many names. I call him Rafael Sabatini.

MR. SCHMITT: Who?

JIM: "I was born with the gift of laughter and a sense that the world is mad."

MR. SCHMITT: How do you educate a boy like that?

LOUISE: Love.

AUSTIN: He loves saying stuff like that. I think it's cool.

JIM: Everything will wear away but this, my sword.

(Jim picks up a pencil off the desk.)

MR. HOFFMAN: I don't want you writing about me.

(Jim quietly brandishes the pencil.)

JIM: I will write about you.

(Mr. Schmitt points at Mr. Hoffman.)

MR. SCHMITT: I'll ask you to leave in a year's time, Alan. After a boy finally comes to me.

(Jim addresses Mr. Hoffman:)

JIM: When you're dying, you'll write to me.
MR. HOFFMAN: I don't feel understood.
JIM: I won't answer the letter.
LOUISE: You'd better go.
MR. HOFFMAN: I will survive many scenes like this.
MR. SCHMITT: Did you hear my wife? Get out.

(Mr. Hoffman is driven out by Mr. Schmitt.)

I didn't see what he was.
LOUISE: Carl.
MR. SCHMITT: I always see too late.
LOUISE: It's not too late.
MR. SCHMITT: How can you say that?
LOUISE: I do say it!
MR. SCHMITT: I killed our son! Nothing can change that.
LOUISE: You've been so sad.
MR. SCHMITT: I didn't see him.
AUSTIN: It was snowing.
JIM: It was snowing
LOUISE: It was snowing. That's what I do at the window. I wait for you.
MR. SCHMITT: How can you forgive me?
LOUISE: Please. In the name of God. Let me forgive you.

(Mr. Schmitt quietly breaks down. Louise comforts him.)

MR. SCHMITT: Our son.

LOUISE *(Indicating Jim)*: He's still here. He can still be saved.

MR. SCHMITT: How?

LOUISE: That's my faith.

(Louise turns to Jim.)

Our son. His name was James. His name was James.

(Mr. Schmitt returns to his desk. Louise returns to the margins of the scene.)

MR. SCHMITT: Mister Quinn.

JIM: Please, Mr. Schmitt . . .

LOUISE: Help him.

JIM: Protect me.

MR. SCHMITT: Mister Quinn, understand I have no idea, not the slightest idea why I'm doing this. I'll die without understanding it.

LOUISE: But I'll understand.

MR. SCHMITT: Jim, I'm going to let you graduate.

(He offers Jim his hand.)

JIM: You are?

AUSTIN: Wow. Uncle Carl.

LOUISE: Thank God.

(Jim shakes his hand.)

JIM: Thank you. This is the moment that you made me, sir. Thank you. Thank you, madam. A lifetime of thanks. Thank you for everything.

(A clock chimes. Music. The Schmitts and Austin fade away. The office vanishes, leaving Jim alone onstage.
From off, we hear Austin distantly calling:)

AUSTIN *(Offstage)*: Jim! Jim!

(Austin reenters, breathless, with a book.)

Jim! I almost forgot! Here.
JIM: What's this?
AUSTIN: A book. You always have a book.
JIM: Thanks.
AUSTIN: Oh. Look at the time. That's it. It's *lights out* for us.

(The lights soften. Austin goes. Evocative music of quiet tension returns. The lights dwindle down to only Jim.)

JIM: When it began, I was fifteen. Do you remember fifteen? You do. For me, it was a special, beautiful room in Hell. *(Referring to his book)* I'll leave this for the next guy.

(He places the book on the ground and, as an afterthought, he places his pencil on top of it, then wanders away, disappearing into the surrounding dark. Only the book and pencil remain.)

END OF PLAY

JOHN PATRICK SHANLEY is the author of numerous plays, including *Doubt, a parable* (winner of the Pulitzer Prize and Tony Award for Best Play), *Outside Mullingar* (Tony Award nomination for Best Play), *Danny and the Deep Blue Sea, Beggars in the House of Plenty, Dirty Story, Where's My Money?, Four Dogs and a Bone, Defiance* and *Storefront Church*. His sole television outing resulted in an Emmy nomination for *Live from Baghdad* (HBO). In the arena of film, *Moonstruck* garnered him an Academy Award for Best Original Screenplay. Mr. Shanley wrote and directed both *Joe Versus the Volcano* and *Doubt*; the latter earned five Oscar nominations, including Best Adapted Screenplay. In 2008, the Writers Guild of America recognized Mr. Shanley's contribution to film with a Lifetime Achievement Award.